THIS BOOK BELONGS TO

IF YOU LIKED THIS CONTENT
LEAVE ME A GOOD REVIEW.

I THANK YOU
VERY MUCH

YOU CAN FIND ME AS

NATY BOOKS

www.ingramcontent.com/pod-product-compliance
Lightning Source LLC
Chambersburg PA
CBHW082137290526
45794CB00008B/3074
9798871158401